Len Hutton

A Pictorial Biography

Len Hutton
A Pictorial Biography

By David Lemmon

With a foreword by
Trevor Bailey

COLLINS & BROWN

First published in Great Britain in 1990
by Collins & Brown Limited
Mercury House
195 Knightsbridge
London SW7 1RE

A CIP catalogue record for this book is available from the
British Library

ISBN 1 85585 097 4

Conceived, edited and designed by Collins & Brown
Limited, Mercury House, 195 Knightsbridge, London,
SW7 LRE

Editor: Colin Ziegler
Design and DTP by Rupert Wheeler

Typeset by The Setting Studio, Newcastle.
Reproduction by The Bath Press, Avon.
Printed and bound in Great Britain by The Bath Press, Avon

Contents

Foreword

by Trevor Bailey

I bowled against Sir Len Hutton on numerous occasions, because, in addition to the two annual county fixtures, he opened for the Players at Lord's. We were also regularly in opposition for two matches at the Scarborough Festival and on the same side for the game against the tourists. This meant, obviously, that I saw him make a vast number of runs as he understandably relished the Essex and the Gentlemen's attacks. In addition, I had the honour of opening the innings for England with him on several occasions and going on three major tours with him, two of which were under his command, including one when I was his vice-captain. As a result I came to know him well as a batsman, as a skipper and as a person.

One unforgettable moment was when I arrived at the ground to find Len in the nets, although he was at the time not out with a century to his credit. It turned out that he had not been entirely happy with his driving on the previous day which, as one of those who had suffered, had seemed remarkably effective to me. Like his successor for Yorkshire and England, Geoff Boycott, he was absolutely dedicated to the job of making vast quantities of runs and possessed the skill, technique and concentration required. The difference between them was that Len had exceptional skill and elegance so that he was never dull to watch and, indeed, could make even the forward defensive positively beautiful. Bowling at Len was an education which taught me many things, especially in my early days when I lacked the control which is essential for any fast medium seamer. Firstly, he made so few errors that to obtain his wicket usually required an exceptional ball. Secondly, he seldom missed punishing anything slightly loose. Thirdly, he had the ability from time to time to hit the good ball to the boundary and, finally, he was always able to keep the score ticking over by his precise placement of singles. My most satisfying delivery at Len was a perfect full toss immediately after the luncheon interval

Trevor Bailey was an integral part of Len Hutton's sides which both regained and retained the Ashes, and he was vice-captain to Hutton on the 1953-54 tour of The West Indies. On that tour he played magnificently, particularly in the final Test in Jamaica when he took 7 for 34 in the first West Indian innings and was Hutton's opening partner. He was one of England's greatest all-rounders and is now one of the BBC's Test Match Special team

during the Scarborough Festival. I had discreetly substituted an orange for the ball. The contents covered him and the prospect of a subsequent cleaning bill clearly worried him.

Unlike the majority of great players, though Tom Graveney and Graeme Pollock were also exceptions, Len's initial movement was forward rather than back and across, which was one of the reasons why he was such a magnificent front foot driver, the most elegant I have seen; why he seldom hooked and why he habitually played slow bowling from the crease. It also explains why he was relatively happier against the ball that left the bat than the one coming into him and why he used me as an opener.

Although Len's career figures are quite outstanding, I have always maintained that they would have been far more impressive if the war had not intervened and caused him to miss six years when he would have been in his prime. It is true that in the immediate post war years there were some easy runs to be picked up on the county circuit; but very big innings, certainly by the fifties, had begun to take their toll, making him very tired both mentally and physically. He had to drive himself to go on after that almost obligatory hundred, whereas in his mid-twenties it would have simply been a stepping stone towards another record.

Batting with Len was also a fascinating and rewarding experience. He always seemed to have so much time, even against fast bowling, and he made it all appear so easy, while he was also a wonderful judge of the single. Equally he knew when not to run, as I discovered at Sabina Park when I opened with him. Len immediately took a single off their one genuinely fast bowler, King, in his first over, and for the next eight I spent my time weaving and ducking as the bouncers flew past my head, sometimes as many as four in an over. At the other end, Len simply chuckled and smiled as he stroked the occasional two and four, and he went on to make a double hundred which contained only one false stroke. He could bat.

The bad, or very difficult pitch provides the supreme test for a batsman and Len was the finest player in these conditions that I encountered. On a near impossible Australian 'sticky' at Brisbane in 1950, when England declared at 68 for 7 and Australia closed their second innings at 32 for 7, I spent fifteen fascinating minutes at the crease with him as he demonstrated how to drop dead at his feet a near half-volley that had reared chest high. In our second innings he made a superlative undefeated 62. I have felt that if he had opened the innings in this match, we might well have won it.

Len was appointed captain of England because he was the finest batsman in the land, possessed a deep knowledge of the game (the result of having been weaned on Yorkshire cricket in the thirties) and was strongly supported by the popular press. But, being a professional, he was only grudgingly received by many of the game's hierarchy, who were still blissfully unaware of the social revolution that was taking place. He proved to be a highly successful, very shrewd, undemonstrative and rather remote leader, and a brilliant tactician. He waged his international campaigns with ruthless efficiency and did not encourage fraternization with the enemy. His assessment of opposing batsmen was outstanding, as, too, was his judgement of when to switch from attack to defence. He had no time for batsmen who lost their wickets as a result of an extravagant stroke and he expected accuracy from his bowlers. He was, however, prepared to allow those whose judgement he trusted to set their own fields.

Personally, I enjoyed playing under Len as in many respects our outlook was so similar. During our long association we never had a cross word and he was always willing to accept advice. However, some players found him hard to understand, while he himself found difficulty in appreciating the romantic.

A quiet, careful, private, rather shy man, Len probably modelled himself on Herbert Sutcliffe, who raised the status of the professional cricketer in the same way that Henry Cotton did for the golf professional. Len applied the same careful and calculated approach to his business as he did to his batting, pursuing money with the same dedication as he did runs; so that it came as no surprise when he did very well. Wealth fascinated him, and he was certainly the only cricketer I have known who turned to the stocks and shares before the sports pages. The cares of captaincy made him retreat still further into himself, and he never mixed easily, but he possessed a decided sense of humour and had knack of delivering, sotto voce, some succint comments which were as dry as well chilled vintage Sancerre.

Introduction

Sir Leonard Hutton

On 7 May 1990, the final day of the four-day county championship match between Surrey and Lancashire at The Oval, Neil Harvey Fairbrother, the Lancashire left-hander, went out to continue an innings which had begun on the Saturday and in which he already had 311 runs to his credit. Fairbrother added 55 to his overnight score before being caught at mid-on in the last over before lunch. His innings of 366 was not only the highest score of his career, the highest of the season, and the third highest in the history of first-class cricket in England; it was also the highest score ever made at The Oval, beating by two runs a record that had stood for 52 years.

Few in the cricket world were willing to accept Fairbrother's record score, good as it was, as being the equal in quality or significance to the old record which had been established in a Test match between England and Australia by a man who was the greatest opening batsman of his era, and one of the finest and most successful captains that England had ever known - Sir Leonard Hutton.

Hutton's first-class career had ended in 1955, but he had become part of the folklore and legend of the game, recognized, admired and respected even by many who had never seen a game of first-class cricket.

He was born at Fulneck, near Pudsey, on 23 June 1916. He was, from an early age, as passionate about cricket as his father and his three elder brothers. He was not sent to Fulneck Boys' School because his parents would have been unable to afford the fees. He went instead to Littlemoor Council School in Pudsey, and it was here that he played some of his first cricket: but it was with the famous Pudsey St Lawrence Club, which he joined at the age of twelve, that his talent was first noted. Within a year of joining them he was in the Yorkshire county nets under the watchful eye of George Hirst, the great all-rounder, who spent the spring helping Yorkshire hopefuls before taking up his coaching job at Eton.

FACING PAGE *Neil Harvey Fairbrother hit 366 for Lancashire against Surrey at The Oval in May 1990, so beating by two runs Len Hutton's record which had been set in 1938. But Hutton's score remains the highest ever made by an Englishman in a Test match and the second highest score in the history of Test cricket.*

Hutton could have left school in 1930 at the age of fourteen, and he was certainly encouraged to become a professional cricketer. But his parents were anxious that he should learn a trade in what were difficult times and they insisted he further his education by spending a year at Pudsey Grammar School.

One of those who had encouraged Hutton to go to the Yorkshire nets was Herbert Sutcliffe, the Yorkshire and England opening batsman, who was deeply impressed by the young lad's talent and helped him in every way.

LEFT *Herbert Sutcliffe was opening partner to both Jack Hobbs and Len Hutton. He exerted a great influence on Hutton whom he predicted would play for England. In this picture, Sutcliffe has suffered the rare fate for him of being bowled in a match between Yorkshire and Kent at Tonbridge.*

In 1934, at the age of seventeen, Hutton made his first-class debut. He was the youngest cricketer to play for Yorkshire since 1889 and, in his eagerness to get off the mark, he ran himself out for 0. His Test career was also to begin with a duck three years later.

Hutton played sixteen first-class matches in 1934 and hit 863 runs, averaging 33.19. He hit the first of his 129 first-class centuries at Worcester on 26 July.

In spite of missing much of the 1935 season through injury, Hutton earned a regular place in the Yorkshire side in 1936, completed a thousand runs in the season and was awarded his county cap. The following year he won his first Test cap, and a great international career had begun. It was in 1937, too, that he hit the first of the eight centuries he was to score at The Oval.

ABOVE *Len Hutton began his first-class career in 1934, the same season that saw Jack Hobbs, 'The Master', retire from first-class cricket. As a boy, Hutton read a book by Hobbs which fired his imagination so much that he was determined to become proficient at cricket. Hutton was to succeed Hobbs as England's number one and so take on his mantle as the master. Hobbs was the first professional cricketer to receive a knighthood; Hutton became the second.*

RIGHT *The ground at New Road, Worcester, where Len Hutton hit the first of his 129 first-class centuries. Surprisingly, Hutton was to play on the ground only three more times in the next twenty-one years, and he did not hit another century there. Invariably, the Worcester ground is flooded by the tributaries of the Severn each spring, a flooding which gives the pitch a character all of its own.*

What distinguished Hutton from other batsmen was the purity of his technique. In sport or art, the mastery of technique is in itself a thing of beauty. Such beauty was and still is apparent in the ice-dancing of Torvill and Dean and when one listened to David Oistrakh playing the violin. It was immediately recognizable, too, in the batting of Len Hutton. He was the complete stylist. He had such mastery of the textbook that he played every stroke to perfection. He was unhurried and graceful in movement, and one did not need to see him hit boundaries to know that one was in the presence of greatness. The style was the man, the bat an extension of arm and body. It was not simply a question of grace and beauty, but of fusion and wholeness.

If Hobbs is generally accepted as the greatest of English professional batsmen, then Hutton stands alongside Hammond

ABOVE *The Oval was to become a ground most dear to Len Hutton. He scored the first of his eight centuries for Yorkshire against Middlesex in a special champion county versus runners-up challenge match at the end of the 1937 season. A year later, The Oval was to be the scene of his famous 364 against Australia. The photograph shows the capacity crowd that watched that innings. The South London ground was to witness the three great landmarks in Hutton's career.*

ABOVE *When Len Hutton arrived in first-class cricket, the greatest English batsman in the game was Wally Hammond. In March 1933, Hammond hit 227 for England against New Zealand at Christchurch, and he followed this within a week with an innings of 336 not out in the second Test at Auckland. This remained a record until Hutton's innings at The Oval in 1938 by which time Hammond, having become an amateur, was England's captain.*

19

LEFT *Denis Compton batting for Middlesex against Essex at Chelmsford in 1938. Compton made his Test debut in the same series as Hutton. Their careers crossed and recrossed, the champions of north and south. Compton believed Hutton to be the greatest opening batsman he ever saw and one of the finest stroke-makers of his day.*

and Compton as very, very close to him. Denis Compton's career was to run nearly parallel to Hutton's. If Hammond or Compton were more flamboyant in approach than Hutton, neither had the responsibility of opening the innings, nor had to carry so much on their shoulders as Hutton did towards the end of his career.

Like Compton, Hutton was to see his career severely disrupted by the Second World War. By September 1939, Hutton was a firmly established Test cricketer with a world record to his credit. He had already scored 36 first-class centuries, and he was still only 23 years old. Thirteen days after the outbreak of war, he married Dorothy Dennis whose brother Frank played for Yorkshire between 1928 and 1933. She was to be tower of strength to him in the years that were to follow.

Although Hutton had beaten Bradman's Test record in 1938, the great Australian batsman still straddled world cricket like a Colossus. He had dominated Test cricket in the thirties to such an extent that, even in the 'body-line' series of 1932-33, a form of attack which was devised to blunt him, 'The Don' had averaged 56.50 and topped the Australian batting.

There were doubts as to whether or not Bradman would be fit enough to return to cricket after the war, but he did and once more put England to the sword. There were also doubts as to whether or not Hutton would be able to return to first-class cricket.

From 1939 to 1945, he was a Physical Training Instructor in the army, but, in March 1942, he suffered a serious injury when he fell on his left arm during commando training in the gymnasium. By midsummer he was playing cricket again although he was still in considerable pain.

ABOVE *Don Bradman strode the cricket world like a Colossus in the 1930s. In 1930, as a fourteen-year-old in short trousers, Len Hutton had watched Bradman make his record 334 at Headingley, little realising that he would beat that score eight years later. Hutton admired and learned.*

RIGHT *On 16 August 1941, Hutton appeared for Sir Pelham Warner's XI against R.A.F. at Lord's. He was top scorer with 19, but he was in such pain from an injury that he could not bat in the second innings and did not play cricket again for another twenty months. The scorecard was filled in by a ten-year old worshipper (myself) who was seeing the great man for the first time.*

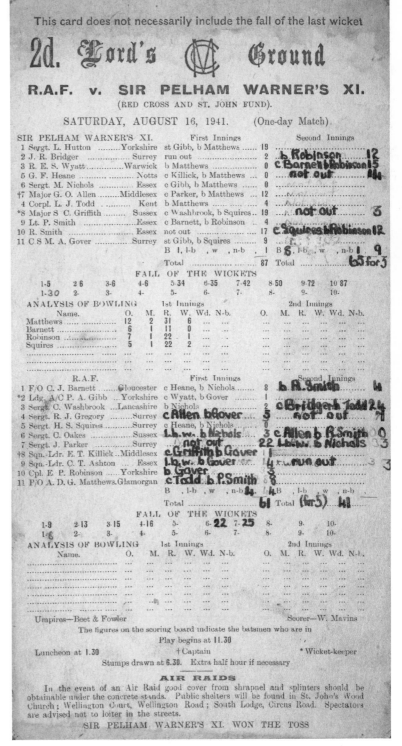

He underwent several operations, and his left arm was in plaster for fourteen months. When it was finally set free it was emaciated and three inches shorter than his right arm. He had never had a strong physique, and had he not had perfect balance and used his feet to such great effect (the qualities which gave him such exquisite timing), it is unlikely that he would have been able to surmount the physical handicap that he now had and been able to continue as the world's leading opening batsman.

He returned to cricket in the Bradford League in 1943, but it was not until 1944 that he was able to play in any of the star-studded matches which were staged at Lord's in aid of charity. It was in these matches that we first saw Keith Miller and in which a generation of schoolboys were able to see players like Hammond, Washbrook and Pope who had previously been no more than cigarette cards.

In May 1945, a match between England and Australia (in reality an England XI versus the Australian Services in Britain) was extended to three days as part of 'Victory Celebrations'. Hutton played in this and the four other Victory Tests which were arranged.

ABOVE RIGHT *The match between 'England' and 'Australia' at Lord's over the Whitsun Bank Holiday, 1945, was extended to three days as part of the Victory Celebrations. Cec Pepper made the winning hit for the Australian side at seven o'clock on the last day, off the fourth ball of the final over. Four more matches were played in the series, two at Lord's, one at Sheffield and one at Old Trafford. Hutton played in all five matches and hit a century in the third match, at Lord's. The series was drawn two each, and the matches were accorded first-class status. Cricket proper had returned.*

RIGHT *Cyril Washbrook became Len Hutton's opening Test partner in the first Test match in England after the war, v India, at Lord's, June 1946. They remained as England's regular opening pair until the match against New Zealand in Christchurch, March 1951. At Ellis Park, Johannesburg, on 27 December 1948, they shared a partnership of 359 against South Africa. This remains a record England opening partnership against any country.*

ABOVE *Reginald Broomhead, a Leeds surgeon, was made a life member of Yorkshire County Cricket Club in recognition of what he had done to make it possible for Len Hutton to continue his cricket career after the war. Bradman, although nearing the end of his career, remained the scourge of England between 1946 and 1948. Hutton, pictured here with Bradman, was dropped from the England side for the third Test at Old Trafford in 1948 after suffering at the hands of fast bowlers Lindwall and Miller. There was a public outcry and this was the only time that Hutton was omitted from an England side, when available, between 1937 and 1955.*

In 1939, Hutton had had three different opening partners in three consecutive matches, but during the Victory Test series in 1945 he established a partnership with Cyril Washbrook of Lancashire that was to last until 1951.

England restarted their Test series after the war with victory over India: but Australia, in 1946-47 and again in 1948, proved far too strong for an England side which had been sapped of energy by the war and which was a blend of tired age and international inexperience. In 1948, Bradman led what was arguably the finest side that Australia have ever fielded.

England followed the defeats by Australia with victory in South Africa, a drawn series against New Zealand and then more defeats, this time by The West Indies, before setting off for Australia again under the captaincy of Freddie Brown. Denis Compton was named as vice-captain of what was a strange mixture of players, many of whom were young and very inexperienced. In fact, the side won the last Test after losing the first four. It was England's first Test victory over Australia for thirteen years.

In 1951, against Surrey at the Oval, Hutton hit his hundredth hundred. He was 61 not out when play ended on the Saturday evening, and, on Monday, 16 July, 15,000 people flocked to The Oval to see if one of the most popular cricketers in the game could reach a famous landmark. 'They were not disappointed,' said Wisden, 'and Hutton achieved his objective with a stroke worthy of the occasion - a drive of Wait sped past cover-point to the boundary.'

In the year that Hutton scored his hundredth hundred, 1951, Yorkshire finished second in the county championship to Warwickshire who were captained by a professional, Tom Dollery. This was most unusual, for it was customary for a county captain to be an amateur even if a professional who was a better player had to be omitted to accommodate him. The distinction between amateur and professional was not to be abolished until the end of the 1962 season.

The England selectors for the series against India in 1952 were Norman Yardley, the Yorkshire captain, Bob Wyatt and Freddie Brown, like Yardley former captains of England, and Les Ames, the most renowned of wicket-keeper batsmen and the first professional cricketer to be named as a Test selector. They broke with tradition in choosing a professional, Len Hutton, as captain. It was a vital decision in the interests of England, although it was not received without criticism, for it meant that in future no man should be picked as leader unless he was worth a place in the side. It had not always been so.

ABOVE *Brian Close was the only other Yorkshire player to be chosen for the 1950-51 tour of Australia along with Hutton. He had made his first-class debut in 1949 and had been picked for England the same season. He was a great admirer of Hutton.*

LEFT *Hutton relaxes on board the SS Stratheden on the way to Australia, September 1950. Had he been able to relax in such a manner more often, Hutton's career may well have lasted longer. He hit 1382 runs and topped the first-class averages on the tour while, in the tests, he averaged 88.83. Only one other England batsman, Reg Simpson (38.77), averaged above 30.*

ABOVE *The Oval was ever a place of good fortune for Len Hutton. In 1951 it was the scene of his hundredth hundred, and a year earlier he had carried his bat through the England innings for 202, only to see his side beaten by The West Indies by an innings and 56 runs. Crowds queued for hours before the gates were opened to see Hutton's innings.*

LEFT *Tom Dollery, Warwickshire's professional captain, sweeps a ball to the boundary against Lancashire, 1951. Wilson is the wicket-keeper; Grieves is at slip. As a professional, Dollery wrote that there were things he dare not do which an amateur could do with impunity. A year after Warwickshire had won the title under Dollery's leadership, Hutton was named as captain of England.*

LEFT *Len Hutton reads telegrams of congratulations after being named as England's first professional captain. He fully justified the selectors' confidence in him as England beat India three-nil in the four-match Test series of 1952.*

RIGHT *Bill Edrich was brought back to the England team after an absence of three years to open the innings with Hutton in the last three Tests of the 1953 Ashes series. He finished second to Hutton in the Test batting averages, and Hutton, like all who were close to the game, greatly admired his tenacity and pluck. The series was watched by 549,650 people, a record for England, and Hutton became the first captain to win a rubber after losing the toss in all five Tests.*

The triumph against India was followed by a home series against Australia in 1953. England had the better of a drawn first Test although they had trailed by 105 runs on the first innings. In the second Test match, Hutton made his fifth and final hundred against Australia. England looked likely to lose the Test when their first four second innings wickets went down for 72, but Trevor Bailey and Willie Watson added 163 and batted until forty minutes before the close to save the game. The next two Tests were drawn, and at the Oval, where Hutton's 82 was the highest score, England won by eight wickets and so recaptured the Ashes after Australia had held them for a record period of almost nineteen years.

England were never to lose a Test series under Hutton's captaincy. He was not a loquacious man, but whatever he said was good sense and good advice. He was not a flamboyant captain just as he was not a flamboyant batsman, but he was thoughtful, with a great tactical awareness, and he prepared himself and his side meticulously. He was a private person, but he had a gentle, quiet humour which was reflected by the twinkle in his blue eyes.

Hutton came to the captaincy through seniority, and the mantle never appeared to rest easily upon him. It did not seem to be something he relished, but his quiet dignity, his modesty and his charm gave him a very special quality that did not mask the fact that he was a very stern opponent and that, like all true Yorkshiremen, his one desire was to win.

In his study of the cricket captains of England, Alan Gibson accepts the criticisms of Hutton, his caution and his slowing of the over-rate. The caution came as much from the circumstances in which he, a professional, was appointed captain of England in a game still ruled by amateurs as from his own natural caution; and the slowing of the over-rate grew from his desire to keep his fast bowlers fresh and active. But Gibson wrote that if he were pressed to say whom he thought to be the best captain England has ever had, he would plump for Sir Leonard. Few would disagree with him.

Hutton was exhausted by his efforts in the Caribbean and by the difficulties on and off the field that he had encountered. He was forced to spend much time recuperating, and he failed to reach a thousand runs in an English season for the first time since 1935. In the first series to be played against Pakistan, in 1954, David Sheppard led England in two Test matches while Hutton was absent. Behind the scenes there were moves to have Sheppard named as captain to take the side to Australia, for the amateur lobby was still strong; but public opinion was firmly on Hutton's side.

The outstanding success in Australia meant that Hutton's position was now unassailable, and he was appointed

The captain and his troops are taught a new card game on the eve of their tour to Australia, September 1954. Wardle, Statham and Loader look down upon Graveney, Hutton and Evans who are being instructed by Mr A.P. Norman. They were to return from Australia as national heroes.

Brian Statham made his England debut in March 1951, but he played in only one Test match in the 1953 series against Australia. He was, however, England's leading strike bowler in the series against The West Indies in the Caribbean the following winter, even though injury ruled him out of the final Test. This tour marked one of Hutton's greatest achievements.It was fraught with problems, but, having lost the first two Tests, Hutton led his side back to draw the series. He averaged 96.71.

captain of England for all five Test matches against South Africa in 1955, a mark of confidence that had been shown to none of his predecessors. Under a rule just passed, he was made an Honorary Cricket Member of the MCC. What was not known was that he had played his last Test match. He was stricken with lumbago early in the season, played in just ten championship matches for Yorkshire and was obviously far from fit. He soon announced his retirement from first-class cricket.

The great sadness was that the strain of captaincy and continuous Test cricket had taken its toll on him and forced him into retirement earlier than might have been expected.

A year after his retirement, Hutton was knighted for his services to cricket, an honour that was begrudged him by no one. He covered Test matches for The Observer newspaper and moved south, eventually, to Kingston in Surrey in order to be closer to his business interests and, more importantly, because he found the climate better for his health: but he never ceased to be a Yorkshireman.

He was a Test selector from 1975 to 1976, and Gooch, Edmonds and Brearley were among those who made their Test debuts in this period.

Hutton was not a man given to great guffaws of laughter. He was essentially a private man, but a man of gentle humour and a dignity that was never pompous. To be with him was to be with a man who showed interest in what one was doing and who offered kind words of encouragement. He was a man who gave shafts of light.

It was appropriate that his last public appearance at a cricket match should be at The Oval Test match between

The 129th and last century of Len Hutton's career was made at Trent Bridge, Nottingham, 27 June 1955. He hit 194 for Yorkshire against Nottinghamshire. The last 94 runs came in 65 minutes.

ABOVE *At the beginning 1990, Sir Leonard Hutton accepted the Presidency of Yorkshire County Cricket club. It was a proud day for both Hutton and the Club, but, in truth, it had come too late for his health was failing.*

England and India in August 1990, for it was The Oval that had witnessed his three greatest deeds and been such an important and cherished part of his life.

He died in Kingston Hospital, Surrey, following an operation for a ruptured aorta on Thursday, 6 September 1990. That day, Yorkshire were playing the Yorkshiremen at Scarborough. It was a coincidental but fitting salute to one whom Brian Walsh, the Yorkshire chairman, called "a boy's hero and the man every cricketer longed to be. If one is lucky, men like Len Hutton emerge once in a generation."

His death, like that of Lord Olivier a year earlier, affected people beyond the confines of his chosen profession. There was an awareness that a period of history had come to an end and that a greatness had passed from among us.

Chapter One

The Young Yorkshire Cricketer

In the 1930s, Yorkshire dominated the county championship. Between 1931 and 1939, they won the title seven times and provided the nucleus of the England side. The seeds of this dominance had been sown as far back as 1883 when Lord Hawke became the county captain. He revolutionized the county club, bringing it discipline, spirit and pride.

Len Hutton began his first-class career batting at number five, but by the end of the 1934 season he was opening the innings and was to become Sutcliffe's regular partner.

The position of Sutcliffe's opening partner was initially filled by Arthur Mitchell, a fine utility player who won six Test

LORD HAWKE.
YORKSHIRE

LEFT Lord Hawke was captain of Yorkshire from 1883 until 1910. He created the white rose badge for the county and continued to be the dominant figure in cricket politics after his playing days were over. He was president of the club until his death in October 1938. It was he who created the ethos of the Yorkshire club in which Hutton thrived.

FACING Len Hutton, Yorkshire and England, at the peak of the first part of his career. In 1939, he not only scored 2883 runs, but took 44 wickets at 18.68 runs each to finish tenth in the national bowling averages. His leg-break bowling was virtually to disappear after the war.

OVERLEAF In 1932, against Essex at Leyton, Herbert Sutcliffe and Percy Holmes created a world record with an opening partnership of 555. The previous record had been held by two other Yorkshiremen, Brown and Tunnicliffe. Holmes was nearing the end of his career when the record was established and he retired in 1933. Hutton was to fill the vacancy he left.

caps, or by Wilf Barber. By the 1936 season, Hutton was firmly established and, in the opinion of Lord Hawke and Brian Sellers (the Yorkshire captain), on the verge of the England side.

The Yorkshire team that Hutton moved into was rich in character and proud of its eminence. They recognized the quality of the young man who had joined them, and he was treated with kindness and encouragement.

H. VERITY

M. LEYLAND

Brian Sellers was one of the greatest captains county cricket has ever known. In his nine years as captain he took Yorkshire to the title six times. He took over the leadership during the 1932 season when the regular captain, Greenwood, became unavailable. He was a fearless fielder and a fierce competitor. He demanded total commitment from his side and raised the standard of Yorkshire's out-cricket to one unmatched by any other county. Hutton said of him that when he had the scent of victory he was like a house set on fire. His influence on Hutton as a captain and as a cricketer was profound.

Hedley Verity became one of Hutton's closest friends and was an immense help to the young professional, particularly when he was struggling for form and to win a regular place in the side. Verity's career lasted only nine years, 1930-1939, but he was the greatest slow left-arm bowler of his day. He took all ten wickets for 10 runs against Nottinghamshire in 1932. In his last first-class match, against Sussex at Hove in 1939, he took 7 for 9 as the home side were bowled out for 33. He was killed in action in Italy four years later.

Equally helpful to Hutton in his formative years was Maurice Leyland, a solid and brilliant left-hander who was to become county coach. He and Hutton shared many memorable stands, but the most historic was their second wicket partnership of 382 for England against Australia at The Oval in 1938. It remains a record.

ABOVE *Appropriately enough, Hutton's first century for Yorkshire in Yorkshire was at the county headquarters at Headingley, Leeds. He made 131 against Middlesex there in 1935. He hit 15 of his 129 centuries on the ground, more than he made anywhere else.*

BELOW *Bill Bowes was one of five Yorkshire cricketers to play for England at The Oval in the Test match against Australia in 1938. Hutton, Leyland, Verity and Wood, the wicket-keeper who was making his Test debut at the age of 40, were the others.*

Len Hutton hit his first first-class century in 1934, and he added two more in the next two seasons. His blossoming came in 1937 when he scored ten hundreds, and he followed this with six in fewer innings in 1938. In all, he hit 129 centuries on 43 different grounds, ranging from Bradford to Bloemfontein.

While Lord Hawke first captained and then ruled the Yorkshire club, the legend grew that England could only be strong when Yorkshire was strong. In the 1930s, thirteen Yorkshire cricketers represented England, and in the famous victory over Australia at The Oval in 1938 there were five Yorkshiremen in the side.

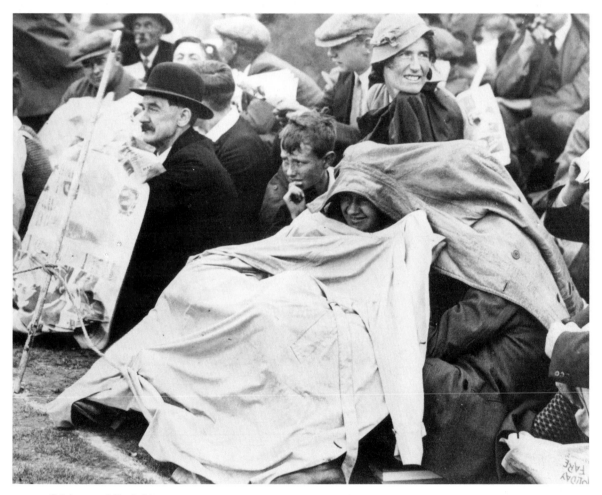

ABOVE *Cricket, and Yorkshire cricket in particular, had a passionate following in the thirties when people were willing to wait with more patience and less comfort than they are today.*

OGDEN'S CIGARETTES

H. SUTCLIFFE

OGDEN'S CIGARETTES

L. HUTTON

ABOVE *Sutcliffe, whose career was neatly condensed between the wars, had been featured on cigarette cards since 1926. In 1938, Hutton joined him in an Ogden series.*

ABOVE RIGHT *Herbert Sutcliffe pulls a ball to the leg-side boundary during his innings of 61 for Yorkshire against Essex at Ilford, 30 June 1937. Hutton hit 124 and shared an opening stand of 109. Hutton's century was his fourth in successive county innings and helped him to hold his place in the England side against New Zealand after his 'duck' in the first Test.*

Yorkshire drew large crowds wherever they went, and rival counties cherished a victory over Yorkshire as the summit of their achievement. The white rose county had a seemingly unending stream of quality players who were jealous of the county's record and instilled with the desire to win. Sellers, captain from 1932 to the war, lived by the maxim that one got nothing for being second. His team shared that belief.

When the Second World War broke out in 1939, Yorkshire had just won the county championship for the third year in succession, and Len Hutton, 23 years old, was at the peak of his career. In that last season before the war he scored 2,883 runs, more than any other batsman in the country, and his average of 62.67 was only fractionally below Wally Hammond's at the top of the national batting averages. He was also established as a Test cricketer of world renown.

The Yorkshire side of the 1930s had achieved success because of inspired captaincy, brilliant fielding, quality batting, bowling in depth, and a unity of spirit and mutual respect which were the envy of others. The effect of these players and this unity of spirit on Hutton in the years to come was immeasurable.

38

Chapter Two

The Test Cricketer 1937-1939
Record Years

There had been those, Sutcliffe among them, who would have selected Hutton as a member of G.O.B. Allen's side to tour Australia in 1936-37 in spite of his limited experience. That side had had considerable difficulty in finding a regular opening pair, so it was no surprise when Hutton was chosen for the first Test against New Zealand in 1937. He had begun the season in splendid form, hitting 161 for Yorkshire against MCC in the opening match of the season at Lord's.

LEFT *Walter Robins, the Middlesex skipper, was named as captain of England against New Zealand in 1937. He came in for criticism in the first Test match when he decided to open his innings with J.H. Parks and Len Hutton, both of whom were making their Test debuts, even though Charlie Barnett was in the side. Hutton scored 0 and 1, but was retained for the rest of the series. Jim Parks never played in a Test match again. Robins was a Test selector when Hutton was dropped for the only time, in 1948, and he was later to lead a lobby which wanted Sheppard rather than Hutton as England captain.*

ABOVE *Walter Hadlee falls on his wicket as he tries to avoid a ball from Arthur Wellard in New Zealand's first innings of the second Test match at Old Trafford, July 1937. Hadlee had scored 93. This was the match in which Hutton hit his first Test century. Freddie Brown and Wally Hammond are at slip, and Les Ames is behind the stumps. Brown was Chairman of the selectors when Hutton's side regained the Ashes in 1953.*

FACING *Martin Donnelly of New Zealand began his Test career at Lord's in June 1937, as Hutton did. Like Hutton, he began with a 'duck', and, also like Hutton, he was to exact his revenge, hitting 206 against England at Lord's in 1949.*

Compton and Washbrook were among those who made their Test debuts in the series against New Zealand in 1937, and more new faces were to appear in Test cricket when Australia, led by Don Bradman, arrived in 1938. Edrich, Sinfield and Wright made their debuts in the first Test, and Price and Wood, both wicket-keepers, were used later in the series when Ames was injured.

The Test match at Trent Bridge was drawn, as was the second at Lord's where Hutton failed in both innings. The Australians had a narrow escape in their match against Yorkshire at Bramall lane, Sheffield, for Yorkshire, needing 150 to win, were 83 for 3 when rain ended the match. Rain completely washed out the third Test due to be played at Old Trafford, the match being abandoned without a ball being bowled. That match had been scheduled to begin on 8 July, and the fourth Test, at Headingley, began a fortnight later. Unfortunately, in the intervening period, Yorkshire suffered their first defeat of the season, against Middlesex at Lord's. It was not so much the defeat, but the toll that the match took on England and Yorkshire. On a spiteful pitch, Gibb was struck on the head and injured, Hutton sustained a broken finger and Leyland a broken thumb. All three would have been

PLAYER'S CIGARETTES

C. J. BARNETT

Charlie Barnett was Hutton's opening partner when England played Australia at Trent Bridge, Nottingham, June 1938. They shared an opening stand of 219. Barnett hit 126, and Hutton 100. At lunch on the first day, Friday, 10 June, England were 169 for 0, with Barnett 98 not out. He completed his century on the first ball after lunch, the nearest that any batsman has come to scoring a century for England before lunch on the first day.

LEFT *Wally Hammond leads his team onto the field after declaring the England innings closed at 658 for 8 at 3.15 on the second day of the first Test, 1938. Barnett, Hutton, Paynter (216 not out) and Compton all hit centuries. McCabe played a marvellous innings of 232 but Australia were forced to follow on. Brown and Bradman hit hundreds to save the game. This was Hammond's first match as England's captain. He had turned amateur after the 1937 season. The photo is particularly poignant in that he is followed onto the field by Farnes, Verity and Ames. Both Farnes and Verity were to be killed in the war.*

in the England side for the Headingley Test, but all three were forced to withdraw.

It had been decided that the fifth Test match, at The Oval, was to be played to the finish. It was a 'timeless' test. In the event it was over in four days.

RIGHT *Doug Wright, the Kent leg-spinner, made his Test debut in 1938. At Headingly, he took 2 for 38 and 3 for 26. His five wickets were Bradman, McCabe, Brown and Hassett twice, a formidable haul, but England lost by five wickets. This was the one Test match in 1938 in which Hutton was unable to play through injury. Wright was to miss the last Test at the Oval because of injury.*

LEFT *Groundsman 'Bosser' Martin watches Bradman and Hammond as they toss up before The Oval Test match in 1938. Hammond won the toss for the forth time in succession. Martin had the reputation for producing the finest wickets in England in the thirties, and his expertise was acknowledged in that he was called to Lord's in 1935 to rid the ground of 'leather-jackets'. In creating a wicket for the 'timeless' Test, he prepared one which the bowlers watered with their tears.*

LEFT *Australia did not possess a strong attack, but Edrich was caught off O'Reilly, at 29. From that point onwards the bat dominated. Hutton cuts a ball during his innings of 364. Ben Barnett is the wicket-keeper and Jack Fingleton is at short-leg.*

RIGHT *Len Hutton is congratulated by Joe Hardstaff Junior, with whom he put on 215 for the sixth wicket, and by Don Bradman after he has passed Bradman's record in an England-Australia Test match.*

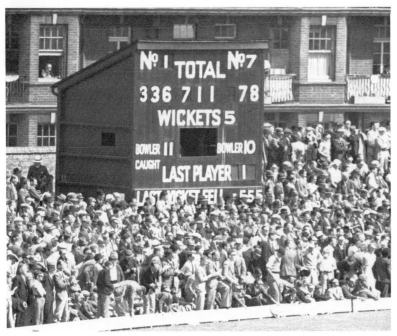

ABOVE *More congratulations for Hutton, this time from Bill Brown. The Australian opener was last out in the Australian first innings so that he was on the field for the first eighteen and a half hours of the match. Hutton's 364 occupied 13 hours 17 minutes and was made out of 770 runs scored while he was at the wicket. He hit 35 fours.*

LEFT *Hutton was 300 not out at the end of the second day and took some time to pass Bradman's record, which he did by square-cutting Fleetwood-Smith for four. The score-board records the historic moment. Hardstaff is number seven.*

RIGHT *'When sorrows come, they come not single spies, But in battalions.' With the England score in excess of 800 and 4 wickets still standing, Don Bradman sustained a flake fracture of the right ankle when bowling and had to be carried from the field. He took no further part in the match, nor in the tour. Fingleton strained a muscle and was unable to bat in either innings. It was these factors which allowed Hammond to declare at tea on the third day with England's score a record 903 for 7.*

L. O'B. FLEETWOOD-SMITH

ABOVE *L. O'B. Fleetwood-Smith conceded 298 runs in his 87 overs, an unwanted record.*

RIGHT *The score-card of the fifth Test match between England and Australia at The Oval in 1938. England's score and their margin of victory, an innings and 579 runs, are among the many records set in this historic match.*

When the MCC team went to South Africa in the autumn of 1938, Hutton was accompanied by three other Yorkshiremen; Yardley, Gibb and Verity. A blow on the head in the match against Transvaal kept Hutton out of the first Test in which Gibb scored 93. He was back for the rest of the series which England won by one match to nil and played in his second 'timeless' test. This was the last game of the series at Durban, and, timeless as it was, it had to be abandoned after ten days as a draw so that the England party could catch the boat home.

The Test series against The West Indies in 1939 was played in an air of crisis with the threat of war ever-present. Nevertheless, it was a highly successful series for Hutton who hit 196 and 16 as England won the first Test at Lord's by 8 wickets.

BELOW *The West Indian attack was spearheaded by the great all-rounder Learie Constantine. He was now 37 years old, and his bowling had lost a little of its pace, but he was still a potent force and a mighty hitter. Here he is seen bowling against Essex at Chelmsford three weeks before the first Test. He took 13 wickets for 91 runs in the match which the tourists won by two wickets.*

ABOVE *Constantine's new ball partner was Martindale, who had a disappointing tour. By playing in the series against West Indies, Hutton had played against all Test playing countries bar India within the space of two years and faced the leading bowlers in the world.*

ABOVE RIGHT *The second Test match at Old Trafford was ruined by rain. Sealy, the West Indian wicket-keeper, skies a ball from Goddard, the Gloucestershire off-spinner, but escapes. Arthur Wood is the England wicket-keeper.*

RIGHT *The third Test match at The Oval was drawn. Hutton hit 73 in the first innings and shared a second wicket stand of 131 with Norman Oldfield, who was playing in his one and only Test match. Hammond hit 43 before becoming one of Constantine's five victims, brilliantly caught at short-leg by Grant, the West Indian skipper.*

There was to be no more Test cricket for seven years, and the first phase of Len Hutton's test career had been brought to an impressive close. In the space of three years, he had played in thirteen Test matches, hit five centuries and three fifties, and in twenty innings, once not out, had scored 1,345 runs, averaging 67.25. The Indian attack was the only one in world cricket which he had not faced, and he had taken centuries off Australia, New Zealand, West Indies and South Africa. That was a mighty achievement for a young man of 23, but, like thousands, he now faced a trying period.

BELOW *In the second innings, Hutton and Hammond scored 264 in three hours for the third wicket, which was a world Test record at the time. Hammond hit 135 and Hutton 165 not out. Hutton is seen here hooking Johnson to the boundary. It was a shot he was to play less often after the war, which broke out two weeks after this match ended in a draw.*

Chapter Three

Testing Time 1946-1951

When first-class cricket resumed in 1946, Len Hutton was 30 years old and his left arm was two inches shorter than his right. Operations had been followed by massage and therapy and, although he had been invalided out of the army in the summer of 1942, he had continued to work for the Royal Engineers as a civilian employee.

The war had sliced his career in half. He had been dubbed a slow batsman because of his marathon 364 at The Oval when time was of no importance, but he had shown tremendous flair the following season in all types of cricket. Now, seven years on, he was faced with the prospect of re-establishing himself and overcoming a physical handicap. A modest series against India in 1946 suggested that he was not the Hutton of old.

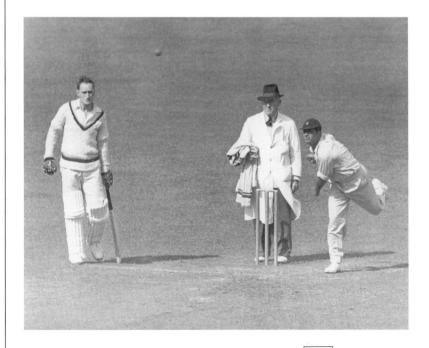

LEFT *India provided England's opposition in the first Test series after the war. Their outstanding cricketer was the all-rounder Mankad, a teasing slow left-arm bowler and a dogged batsman. Hutton's highest score in the three-match series was 67, but he passed 1,500 runs in all matches and hit four centuries in the season. The following winter he went to Australia with the England party.*

51

That England would struggle in Australia was known before the party set sail, and the MCC undertook the series reluctantly. Hammond, James Langridge, Voce and Peter Smith were at the veteran stage and, after the war years, several of the side were less than fit for a tour of Australia. The weaknesses in bowling were apparent before the first Test which was lost by an innings and 332 runs, and another innings defeat followed in the second Test.

The fourth Test was drawn. Compton hit a century in each innings, as did Arthur Morris. Miller made 141 not out, and Hutton played two outstanding innings of 94 and 76. The match was played in perpetual heat and humidity, the temperature often reaching 105.

BELOW *England avoided defeat in the third Test match at Melbourne in January 1947. In the first Test they had fallen foul of the all-round skill of Miller, and the batting of Bradman, Barnes and Hassett had dominated both matches. McCool, Lindwall and Morris all scored centuries in the third Test, but England put on a spirited show. Miller was somewhat fortunate as he scrambled back to his crease as Evans fumbled the ball, but he was caught by Hammond off Yardley, a surprise bowling success, for 34.*

RIGHT   *Rain fell before the start of the fifth Test in Sydney so that there was always help for the bowlers. Hutton batted splendidly throughout the opening day to reach 122, but he was then taken to hospital with acute tonsilitis and could take no further part in the match which Australia won by five wickets. Their hero was Ray Lindwall, the fast bowler who had emerged as the main threat to England. Lindwall had finished England's first innings in the fourth Test by taking three wickets, all bowled, in four balls, and in the fifth Test he had figures of 7 for 63 and 2 for 46.*

LEFT *Hammond's career ended with the tour of Australia. The 1947 season was one of almost perpetual sunshine and will always be remembered for the deeds of Compton, right, and Edrich, left, who hit 3,816 and 3,539 runs respectively. Hutton hit 2,585 to show that he had now recovered health and form.*

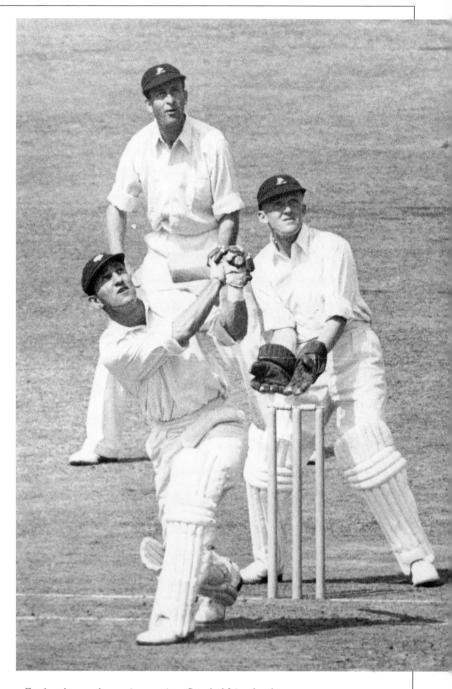

England won the series against South Africa by three matches to nil. Hutton hit a century in the fourth Test and, in the fifth, he and Compton shared a third wicket stand of 98 after two wickets had fallen quickly. Here he hits a ball from Athol Rowan to leg as wicket-keeper Fullerton watches.

In the early months of 1948, England sent a party to the Caribbean to play a five-Test series against The West Indies. The strength of West Indian cricket was grossly underrated, and players of the calibre of Hutton, Compton, Edrich and Bedser were not available. In spite of the absence of these senior players and the presence of four young men; Smithson, Wardle, Tremlett and Laker, the average age of the side was above thirty, and it was led by G.O.B. Allen who was also the manager. He was 45 years old and was never completely fit.

BELOW *South Africa were set to make 451 to win the match and finished 28 runs short with 7 wickets down. Viljoen cuts a ball from Howorth past Hutton in the gully. Evans is the wicket-keeper and Yardley at slip. Mitchell, the non-striker, carried his bat for 189, having hit 120 in the first innings.*

It was known from the outset that the 1948 season was to see the last of Don Bradman in international cricket. It was also known that he led a strong Australian side. But few expected that the side would be as strong as it was, that it would outclass England claiming four of the five Tests and go through the tour unbeaten, winning 23 of its 31 first-class matches.

RIGHT *England went through the tour of the West Indies, 1947-48, without a win in eleven matches. Two of the four Tests were lost. Frank Worrell averaged 147 in the series, and England had had their first taste of the strength of West Indian cricket.*

LEFT *The one England success was off-spinner Jim Laker who took 36 wickets on the tour, 18 in Tests. So desperate was England's plight that Allen cabled home for a batsman to strengthen the side. Hutton had wanted a rest, but he agreed to fly to the Caribbean and help. He played in the last two Tests and hit 578 runs in five matches to top the tour averages.*

LEFT *The Australians arrive at Tilbury, 16 April 1948. Don Bradman waves his hat in greeting. Toshack is behind him and Lindwall is partly obscured by the hat. Miller has his hands on Hassett's shoulders, and either side of Miller are Ring and Johnston. Ian Johnson is next to Hassett with Tallon looking over his shoulder. Barnes has his head bowed while Brown lounges with a book in his hand. Morris is at the back, his head visible over the shoulder of manager K. Johnson who holds a paper. Hamence, Harvey and McCool are in front. Australia has sent no better side to England.*

RIGHT *Bradman leads his side on to the field at Worcester. Hassett and Toshack are alongside him. McCool is just behind them, and Miller and Tallon can be seen in the background. Both Bradman and Morris scored centuries and the Australians won by an innings.*

BELOW *England were beaten by 8 wickets in the first Test match, at Trent Bridge. They were 344 in arrears on the first innings, and their second innings began disastrously when Washbrook attempted to hook a Miller bouncer and was caught behind for 1. Umpire Chester gives the decision while Hutton looks on. Hassett, Barnes, Brown, Tallon and Miller are the fielders.*

Bradford, in May, was the setting for the third match of the Australians' tour which Yorkshire lost by four wickets in a low-scoring match. This was the closest that the tourists came to defeat. They beat a strong MCC side at Lord's at the end of the month, but Hutton was in a class of his own with innings of 52 and 64.

At Lord's, in the second Test match, England began well with Hutton catching both Barnes and Bradman at short-leg. Australia then asserted themselves and made 350 and 416 for 7 declared. England were bowled out for 215 and 186. Hutton was bowled by off-spinner Johnson for 20 in the first innings and was caught at slip by Lindwall for 13 in the second. He looked most uncomfortable; but no England batsman had looked at ease against Australia's pace attack. The selectors issued no formal statement, but they omitted Hutton from the side to play in the third Test at Old Trafford.

Hutton was recalled for the fourth Test, at Headingley, and hit 81 and 57. He was even pressed into service with his leg-breaks on the last day. Australia, set to make 404 in 344 minutes, won by 7 wickets. Bradman made his last century in Test cricket.

BELOW *Edrich fell at 39, but Hutton and Compton added 111 before Hutton was bowled by Miller for 74 in the gathering gloom. Miller bowled five bouncers in eight balls to Hutton and hit him on the left arm. Compton, too, was hit and fell on his wicket as he tried to evade a Miller bouncer. His 184 was his highest score against Australia. Morris and Johnson are at slip, Tallon is the keeper.*

RIGHT *England drew the Old Trafford Test, rain severely interrupting the game after England had led by 142 on the first innings. Australia ended on 92 for 1 with Morris, here playing a ball from Bedser, 54 not out. Edrich is at slip, and Crapp and Young are the leg-side fielders. This is the only Test from which Hutton was ever dropped, and his omission caused an outcry.*

RIGHT *England's humiliation was completed at The Oval in the final match of the series. The match began on the Saturday and they were bowled out for 52. Compton becomes the first of Lindwall's six victims as he turns the ball to Morris at short-leg. Hutton was the only England batsman to reach double figures. He was last out, brilliantly caught on the leg side by Tallon off Lindwall for 30.*

LEFT *Morris and Barnes put on 117 for Australia's first wicket, and Bradman came in shortly before six o'clock. The crowd rose and applauded, and Yardley led the England side in three cheers. Bradman was bowled second ball, and a great Test career was at an end with an average of 99.94.*

LEFT *Edrich is bowled by Lindwall when England bat again, and the home side are on their way to defeat by an innings and 149 runs. Hutton was again top scorer with 64 and was on the field for all but the last 57 minutes of the match.*

BELOW *Hutton's success continued in the home series against New Zealand when he averaged 78.16. In the first Test he hit 101 and, at The Oval, he scored 206 and shared a stand of 218 with Edrich who here cuts a ball past Rabone with Reid looking on. Hutton's third 50 came in 35 minutes. All four Tests were drawn, and this was the last occasion when only three days were allotted to a Test match.*

In the welcoming warmth of South Africa, Len Hutton continued as England's dominant batsman in the successful Test series in which he hit two centuries. He topped the Test match batting averages, and he and Washbrook established their first wicket record at Johannesburg.

Hutton hit 3,429 runs in 1949, the one season in his career when he exceeded three thousand runs, and his twelve centuries equalled what he had achieved in 1939. Only Compton, Edrich and Hayward have scored more runs in a season that Hutton did in 1949, and his 1,294 runs in June remains a record for a calendar month. With Compton still recovering from a knee operation, Hutton now had the responsibility of the England batting firmly on his shoulders for the series against The West Indies in 1950.

LEFT *The West Indian batting was expected to be strong with the three W's; Worrell, Weekes and Walcott, and Everton Weekes gave early evidence of the immense strength with an innings of 304 not out in 5 hours 25 minutes against Cambridge University. Denman is the wicket-keeper. Weekes was to share a stand of 283 in 210 minutes with Frank Worrell in the Nottingham Test, which Hutton missed through an attack of lumbago.*

LEFT *England won the first Test at Old Trafford by 202 runs, but The West Indies created history at Lord's when they beat England in England for the first time. The architects of the victory were the spinners Ramadhin and Valentine.*

RIGHT *Sonny Ramadhin had arrived in England as an unknown quantity, but the mystery bowler bemused England and took 26 wickets in a series in which the home side used 25 players in four Tests. In the final match, at The Oval, Hutton became the only England batsman to carry his bat through a completed innings against The West Indies. He scored 202 not out, and he and Compton, back after his operation, put on 109 for the third wicket; but England still lost by an innings. The West Indies won the series three to one.*

The MCC team which toured Australia under the captaincy of Freddie Brown, 1950-1951, was one of the stranger sides to leave these shores; an uneasy mixture of untried youth and jaded experience. The selectors faced no easy task. Compton's fitness was still in doubt, Washbrook was not available initially for selection, neither Yardley nor Mann was able to accept the captaincy, and Edrich, although it was not known at the time, was under an undisclosed three-year ban for some minor misdemeanour. Six of the original party were immature cricketers, and these were supplemented by Tattersall and Statham who were flown out to bolster the side in the course of the tour. In the midst of adversities (Compton scored only 53 runs in four Test matches) Hutton was a tower of strength, the dominant batsman on either side. His average of 88.83 in the series was the only one above 50 for either side.

In the first Test match, England were caught on a Brisbane 'sticky' wicket. Asked to make 193 to win, they were bowled out for 122. Hutton batted at number eight and came in when six wickets had fallen for 30. He played one of the most memorable innings in Test cricket, scoring 62 not out, out of 92, an exhibition of technical perfection that has rarely been equalled.

The victory at Melbourne was a tremendous boost to English cricket, and the following summer, with Brown still in command, England beat South Africa by three tests to one, with one drawn. Hutton was again in fine form, but the series is best remembered for his being given out for obstructing the field in the final Test. He edged a ball from Rowan into the air and, in trying to prevent it from dropping on his wicket, impeded Endean from taking the catch. More significantly, the series saw the Test debuts of Watson, Graveney and May. A new generation of England batsmen had been born.

England lost the third Test, and in the fourth, in which they were also beaten, Hutton became the first England batsman to carry his bat through a completed innings twice, when he hit 156 not out, out of 272. He scored 79 and 60 not out in the final test which England won. Hutton waves to an ecstatic crowd as he and Compton arrive home.

FACING ABOVE *Wicket-keeper McIntyre catches New South Wales opening batsman Moroney off the bowling of Alec Bedser. Compton, Close and Hutton join in the appeal. Unfortunately, Morris and Miller added 265 for the second wicket. Hutton countered with a century for the MCC, but so suspect was the England batting that he was moved down to number six for the first Test, to bolster the middle order.*

FACING BELOW *Hutton batted at number four in the second Test which England lost by 28 runs. Hutton's 40 was England's top score in the second innings. Reg Simpson made 23 before being bowled by Lindwall. Here he turns a ball from the spinner Iverson to leg where Miller comes close to taking the catch.*

Chapter Four

The Years of Triumph
Captain of England

E ncouraging as the achievements under Freddie Brown had been, the fact remained that the captain had turned 40 and there were younger men more worthy of being in the England side on playing merit. Brown himself was a member of the selection committee, and, although Compton had been his vice-captain on the tour of Australia, 1950-1951, Brown and his fellow selectors opted for Hutton as captain of England. Compton's star had waned, for he had been cruelly troubled by his injured knee and, in truth, exciting batsman that he was, he was not a captain. Hutton's appointment was most popular in the press and to those who followed the game, but it was an historic break with tradition. Ironically, it was a denial of Lord Hawke's prayer in 1925 that no professional should ever captain England, 'for when the day comes when we shall have no more amateurs captaining England it will be a thousand pities'.

LEFT *Hutton's opposing captain in his first series was V.S. Hazare, seen joining him in celebration. Hutton and Hazare topped their sides' batting averages in the series which England won three to nil, with the last match abandoned because of rain.*

FACING PAGE *Hutton's reign as captain began just as a new generation of English batsmen was beginning to emerge. Among them was Tom Graveney who made his Test debut in 1951 and played in all four Tests against India, 1952, Hutton's first series as captain.*

LEFT *Tony Lock was chosen to make his Test debut in the third match, at Old Trafford. It was something of a surprise selection as doubts had been cast upon his bowling action. Hutton hit 104, and India were bowled out twice in a day, for 58 and 82. Lock took 4 for 36 in the second innings, and the first time he touched a ball in Test cricket was when he took a brilliant catch at short-leg to dismiss Mankad off Bedser with only 4 scored.*

RIGHT *The sensation of the series, however, was Freddie Trueman. He took seven wickets at Headingley on the occasion of his debut, including three in eight balls in the second innings, when India lost their first four wickets without scoring a run. He took 8 for 31 in the first innings at Old Trafford and finished the series with 29 wickets in four Tests.*

There was optimism before the arrival of the Australians in 1953, for, as inevitably happens, Australia appeared to be in decline as England were in ascendancy. Hutton's success against India made his position as England's captain impregnable, at least for the time being, but the side itself still had problems. There was no regular opening partner for Hutton. Trueman could not find his form and did not play until the final Test, and Laker and Lock did not force their way into the side until late in the series.

Rain upset England's chances in the first Test after they had batted disappointingly in their first innings; and an heroic stand between Watson and Bailey saved them in the second Test when defeat looked likely. Rain ruined the third Test at Old Trafford, but the match finished in bizarre fashion. Australia led by 42 on the first innings and when they went in for a second time they lost 8 wickets for 35 runs as Wardle took 4 for 5 in seven overs in the last half hour. Australia were on top for most of the fourth Test, in which Bedser passed Grimmett's total of 216 Test wickets to establish a new world record, since broken several times. Ultimately, Australia needed 177 to win in 115 minutes and looked as if they might do it until Trevor Bailey bowled leg-theory and conceded only 9 runs in six overs. So the two sides arrived at The Oval with all to play for.

ABOVE *The outstanding bowling contribution in 1953 came from Alec Bedser, who had been the backbone of the England attack since 1946 and, at times, had carried that attack single-handed. He took a record 39 wickets at 17.48 runs each against Australia in 1953, but a year later he was to lose his place as the obsession for pace took over. A totally dedicated professional, Bedser later served England well as selector and manager.*

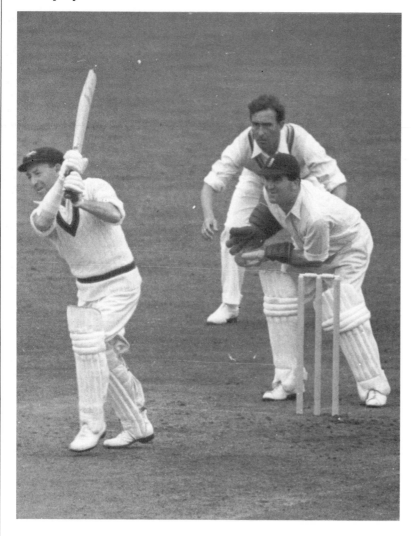

LEFT *Hassett won the toss, and Australia batted first. The Australian captain opened the innings and hit 53. Compton is at slip and Evans behind the stumps.*

ABOVE *Trueman brought about a middle-order collapse, but Davidson and Lindwall halted the slide until Davidson was well caught at slip by Edrich off Laker for 22. Australia were all out for 275.*

RIGHT *There was an early scare in the England innings when Hutton lost his cap. The Australian fielders run forward optimistically, but the cap fell safely over the stumps and Hutton went on to score 82, the highest innings of the match.*

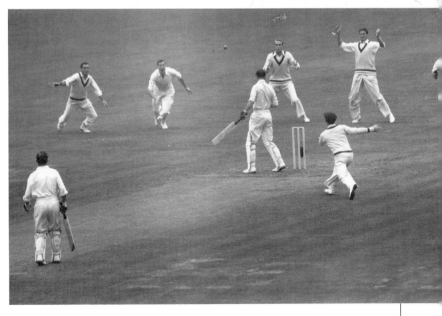

LEFT *Bailey hit 64, and England gained a first innings lead of 31. Hutton soon realised that the batsmen would thrive on pace bowling so he introduced Laker and Lock quickly into the attack. 'That was the move that brought home the Ashes.' Miller is caught at short-leg by Trueman off Laker for 0.*

LEFT *England needed 132 to win and, sadly, Hutton ran himself out for 17 with the score on 24. May puts the ball past a leaping Archer as he and Edrich add 64 for the second wicket.*

FACING ABOVE *May is caught Davidson bowled Miller for 37, but England need only another 44 to win.*

FACING BELOW *Edrich cuts a ball from Johnston, but Hole dives to stop at slip. Edrich finished on 55 not out as England won by 8 wickets.*

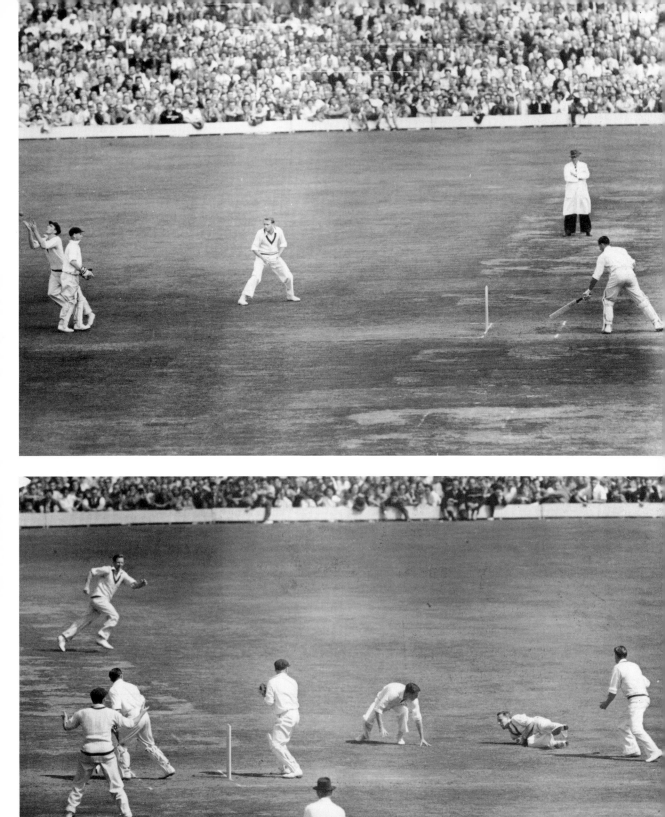

ABOVE *Hassett leads the escape from the field as the celebrating crowds encroach.*

LEFT *The crowds surge towards the pavilion calling for Hutton and the England team.*

RIGHT *England have regained the Ashes for the first time since 1934, and the country rejoices. Hutton is the man of the moment.*

LEFT. *The MCC took the unusual step of appointing Charles Palmer as manager. Palmer (wearing spectacles) is seen here going out to bat with E. Cooper when he was playing for Worcestershire. Palmer was captain/secretary of Leicestershire, and he was to play in his one and only Test match on the 1953-54 tour of the West Indies, for which he had the rather ambiguous role of player/manager while Hutton was captain. Palmer did a difficult job well, but a more experienced and detached manager was needed in a climate which saw an umpire and his wife attacked for a decision he gave and the crowd throwing bottles at the England players in the Test match in Guyana.*

The euphoria that now gripped English cricket was heightened by the fact that England were now to visit The West Indies in what was being described as the championship of the world. It was to prove to be a far from happy tour.

The incidents on the field in the Caribbean and the diplomatic upsets off it took their toll on Hutton, who was also weakened by his herculean efforts in the last three Test matches. He returned to England mentally tired and with a partial break-down of his health. He played little at the beginning of the season, captained England in the inaugural Test match against Pakistan, but was then advised to rest.

ABOVE *Four Yorkshire players; Watson, Trueman, Wardle and skipper Hutton, set out for the tour of the West Indies. England lost the first two Tests but won two of the last three to draw the series in heroic fashion. They owed an immense debt to their captain who finished the series with scores of 169, 44, 30 not out and 205. Gary Sobers made his Test debut in the last match of the series, which was Hutton's last against The West Indies.*

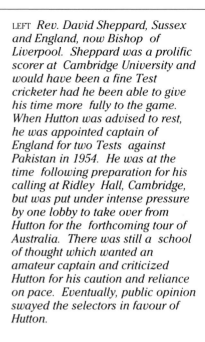

LEFT *Rev. David Sheppard, Sussex and England, now Bishop of Liverpool. Sheppard was a prolific scorer at Cambridge University and would have been a fine Test cricketer had he been able to give his time more fully to the game. When Hutton was advised to rest, he was appointed captain of England for two Tests against Pakistan in 1954. He was at the time following preparation for his calling at Ridley Hall, Cambridge, but was put under intense pressure by one lobby to take over from Hutton for the forthcoming tour of Australia. There was still a school of thought which wanted an amateur captain and criticized Hutton for his caution and reliance on pace. Eventually, public opinion swayed the selectors in favour of Hutton.*

LEFT *Although Sheppard did not make the trip to Australia, the selectors sprang a surprise when they chose Colin Cowdrey of Kent, a 21-year-old batsman with no experience of Test cricket. Cowdrey was a great success. He hit 102 out of 191 in the third Test at Melbourne, which England won, and he maintained that he owed his early success to the help and encouragement given him by Hutton.*

FACING TOP *The series began disastrously for England. Hutton won the toss, asked Australia to bat, and they made 601 for 8 declared. Arthur Morris hits Edrich to leg during his innings of 153. Keith Andrew is the wicket-keeper. He deputized for Evans who was taken ill on the eve of the match. Compton broke a finger while fielding, and England were bowled out for 190 and 257.*

FACING BOTTOM *Following the debacle at Brisbane, England moved to Sydney where they gained a famous victory. Frank Tyson was twice bowled by Ray Lindwall, here, for the first time, for 0, and he was also knocked unconscious by a Lindwall bouncer. But he recovered to bowl at a furious pace and take 4 for 45 and 6 for 85.*

The Australians leap in appeal as Langley, the wicket-keeper, catches Graveney off Johnston for 0, and England are 55 for 3 and facing defeat. That defeat was turned into victory when May and Cowdrey added 116, and Tyson and Statham routed Australia for 184 to give their side a win by 38 runs.

At Melbourne, England trailed by 40 runs on the first innings in spite of Cowdrey's century. May hit 91 and Hutton 42 in the second innings, and England made 279. Tyson produced another thrilling spell of fast bowling. Miller is caught by Edrich for six as the last eight Australian wickets go down for 34 runs. Tyson took 7 for 27, and England won by 128 runs.

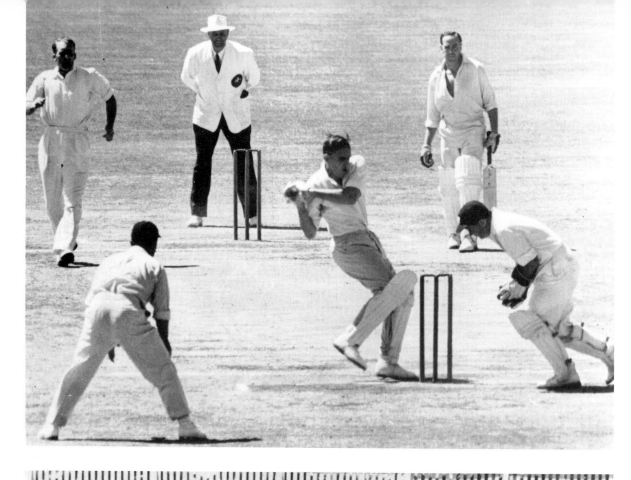

FACING TOP *England won their third Test match in succession at Adelaide. Davidson swats at Wardle and Evans takes the ball, in the Australian second innings, where they were all out for 111.*

FACING BOTTOM *Hutton's trump card, Frank Tyson, in action in the fourth Test, which England won by five wickets. This victory meant that England had won her first series in Australia since 1932-33 and that Hutton had become the first England captain to regain the Ashes and to defend them successfully.*

RIGHT *Richie Benaud, a future Australian captain, was given a torrid time by Hutton and Tyson during the series. The last match, at Sydney, was drawn because of rain although Australia were forced to follow on. The match ended when Hutton bowled Benaud. It was his final gesture against Australia. He played in the two Tests in New Zealand in March of 1955, hitting 53 in the second. A great Test career was at an end.*

Chapter Five

The Elder Statesman

The tour of Australia was a total triumph. Not only had the Ashes been retained in emphatic style, but the tour had passed without incident and the behaviour of the England side on and off the field had been exemplary. The new England selection panel - Allen, Wooller, Sellers and Ames - had no hesitation in appointing Hutton as captain for the series against South Africa. C.B. Fry had been given carte blanche for the triangular series of 1912, but no man since had been appointed captain for an entire series at the beginning of the summer. All seemed well with English cricket for years to come with Hutton in command.

BELOW. *Peter May succeeded Hutton as captain of England. He had been Hutton's vice-captain in Australia and was also understudy to Stuart Surridge, the outstanding captain of the great Surrey side of the 1950s. He was the finest batsman to appear in English cricket since the war, and he modelled his captaincy on Hutton's. Rohan Kanhai is the wicket-keeper.*

However, the tour of the West Indies had exerted considerable mental pressure, and now he returned exhausted from the triumph in Australia and feeling uncertain of his health. He captained the MCC, of which he was now a member, against South Africa in May, fielded on the first day and batted on Saturday evening, receiving a tremendous reception as he went to the wicket. On the Monday, stricken with lumbago, he could not get to the ground. He had no option but to inform the selectors that he would be unable to lead the England side against South Africa. They named Peter May to succeed him and co-opted Hutton onto their selection committee.

It was not simply the cricket that had taken its toll on Hutton's health, but also the extraneous duties that captaincy

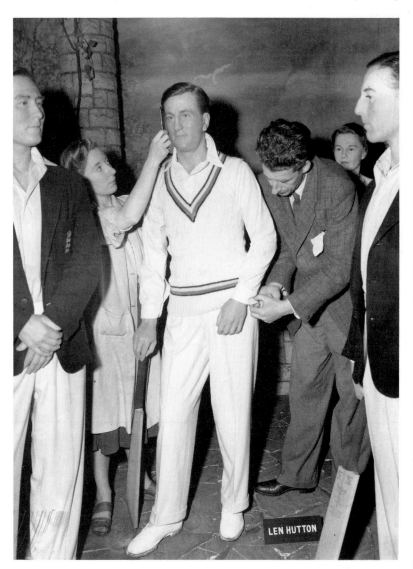

RIGHT *One of the features of fame was a place in Madame Tussaud's wax museum. His model took its place in 1951. Vera Bland and Stanley Wismark complete the finishing touches. The model of Denis Compton stands alongside.*

and fame demanded. It was this side of the job that Hutton, a private and basically shy person, enjoyed least.

Hutton played eleven matches in 1955 with limited success, and, in January 1956, after seeking medical advice, he announced his retirement from first-class cricket.

PLAYER'S CIGARETTES

N. W. D. YARDLEY

ABOVE *Ironically, Norman Yardley, the Yorkshire captain, retired at the end of the 1955 season, and it is probable that Hutton would have been asked to succeed him. Yardley was a kind and gentle person and a fine captain of England in difficult times. He was most supportive to Hutton.*

LEFT *Yardley's successor as captain of Yorkshire was W.H.H. 'Billy' Sutcliffe, the son of Hutton's mentor and former opening partner, Herbert. Like Hutton's sons, the young Sutcliffe had a public school education.*

Although Hutton had been appointed captain of England in 1952, Yorkshire were not to have a professional captain until 1960. The county's successes were to be mingled with some internal strife, and men of the quality of Hutton and Yardley were not easy to replace.

Inevitably, as the years passed there was to be criticism of Hutton. It was suggested that he was too cautious and that he must bear the responsibility for slowing the game to the funereal rate it has reached today. It was also claimed that his playing spinners from the crease had been taken as a model by a generation of cricketers to the detriment of the game. Much of this was nonsense, particularly the latter, for

BELOW *Yorkshire struggled to find an opener to succeed Hutton, but eventually Ken Taylor made the spot his own and won three England caps. He sweeps a ball from Titmus with John Murray and Peter Parfitt looking on.*

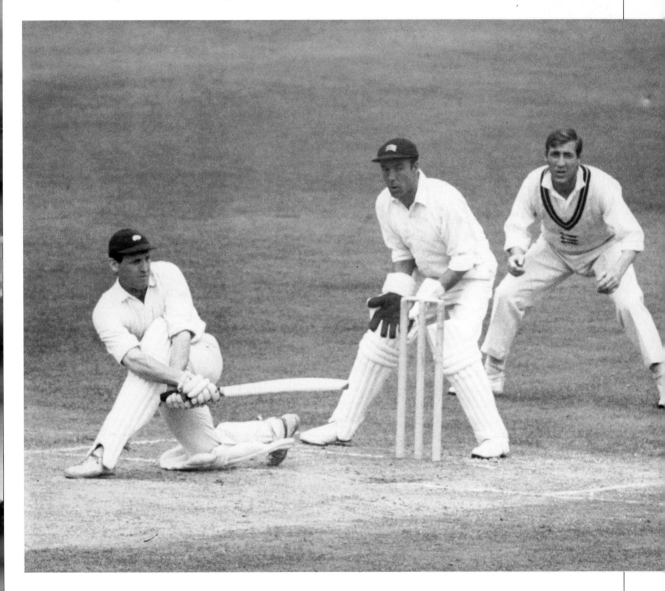

a batsman, if he is good enough, finds his own style and method and does not ape others. Whatever the criticisms, Hutton was recognized as the saviour of English cricket and honours were showered upon him.

Hutton returned to first-class cricket for one match in 1957. It was a bitterly cold Whitsun weekend match between Lancashire and the MCC at Old Trafford, played as part of the festivities to mark the completion of one hundred years of cricket at the ground.

BELOW *Old Trafford, Manchester, where Hutton returned to first-class cricket in 1957 to play for the MCC against the country. Those who saw the match enjoyed a superb display. He hit 76 and 25. 'Flawless in defence, he drove in his most stylish manner'.*

RIGHT *In July 1956, Hutton was knighted by HM the Queen. He is seen at the investiture with Lady Dorothy and his sons Richard and John.*

RIGHT *Ted Dexter, now supremo of English cricket, played in the Old Trafford Centenary match and felt a deep sense of awe to play alongside the man who was the greatest name in cricket. He made 61, and 'Len Hutton, who was **the** great name in those days, came in and said to me, "Keep it up, lad". I was out a couple of balls later.'*

The Hutton name was not lost to Test cricket. Richard Hutton prospered at Repton, a good cricketing school, and played for Yorkshire from 1962 to 1974. He won his blue at Cambridge all three years, 1962 to 1964, and played five times for England in 1971.

Richard Hutton was a fast medium pace bowler and middle-order batsman. He made his Test debut against Pakistan at Lord's in June 1971, took 2 for 36 and hit 58 not out when he opened in the second innings of the rain-ruined match. He played in four more Tests that summer and was bowled by Venkataraghavan for 20 when England met India at Lord's. Engineer is the wicket-keeper. Hutton's short Test career saw him average 36.50 with the bat, hold nine catches and take nine wickets at 28.55 runs each.

ABOVE   *The Test series between The West Indies and Pakistan, which was played in the Caribbean in the first two months of 1958, saw two of Hutton's Test records beaten. In the first Test, at Bridgetown, Barbados, Hanif Mohammad scored 337. He batted for 970 minutes; 193 minutes longer than Hutton's innings at The Oval in 1938.*

RIGHT   *In the Third Test in Kingston, Jamaica, Gary Sobers scored 365 not out, the highest score in Test cricket. It should be said that the Pakistan attack been reduced to only two fit frontline bowlers.*

Sir Leonard Hutton moved south, contributed to *The Observer,* served as a Test selector and prospered in business. He was to see his records beaten, but they have never been eclipsed.

Hutton remained active until the end of his life, attending matches, speaking at dinners and could often be seen at functions concerned with cricket. The game had been and still was his life.

ABOVE *The Oval, 19 August 1953. The greatest of moments. Hutton waves to an ecstatic crowd. England have regained The Ashes after a lapse of 18 years 362 days.*

The Hutton family retains its place in first-class cricket. Simon Dennis, the left-arm medium pace bowler now with Glamorgan, is Sir Leonard Hutton's nephew.

Hutton's death in September 1990, was mourned by all connected with cricket and by many who were not. He stood for a great era in a national game and for the restoration of a national pride. What he accomplished, he did with dedication and without conceit or pomposity. He represented something that was essentially good in life and that went beyond the bounds of the game of cricket.

ABOVE *Three great wicket-keepers, Alan Knott, Les Ames and Godfrey Evans. Ames was first a Test player, and he was a selector on the panel that chose Hutton as England captain. Evans was the England wicket-keeper when the Ashes were regained and retained under Hutton, and Knott was the England keeper when Hutton was selector.*

LEN HUTTON

Statistics

ENGLAND v AUSTRALIA 1953 (1st Test)
Played at Trent Bridge, Nottingham, on 11-16 June.
Toss: Australia.   Result: MATCH DRAWN.

AUSTRALIA

G.B. Hole	b Bedser	0	b Bedser	5
A.R. Morris	lbw Bedser	67	b Tattersall	60
A.L. Hassett*	b Bedser	115	c Hutton b Bedser	5
R.N. Harvey	c Compton b Bedser	0	c Graveney b Bedser	2
K.R. Miller	c Bailey b Wardle	55	c Kenyon b Bedser	5
R. Benaud	c Evans b Bailey	3	b Bedser	0
A.K. Davidson	b Bedser	4	c Graveney b Tattersall	6
D. Tallon+	b Bedser	0	c Simpson b Tattersall	15
R.R. Lindwall	c Evans b Bedser	0	c Tattersall b Bedser	12
J.C. Hill	b Bedser	0	c Tattersall b Bedser	4
W.A. Johnston	not out	0	not out	4
Extras	(B 2, LB 2, NB 1)	5	(LB 5)	5
Total		**249**		**123**

ENGLAND

L. Hutton*	c Benaud b Davidson	43	not out	60
D. Kenyon	c Hill b Lindwall	8	c Hassett b Hill	16
R.T. Simpson	lbw b Lindwall	0	not out	28
D.S. Compton	c Morris b Lindwall	0		
T.W. Graveney	c Benaud b Hill	22		
P.B.H. May	c Tallon b Hill	9		
T.E. Bailey	lbw b Hill	13		
T.G. Evans+	c Tallon b Davidson	8		
J.H. Wardle	not out	29		
A.V. Bedser	lbw b Lindwall	2		
R. Tattersall	b Lindwall	2		
Extras	(B 5, LB 3)	8	(B 8, LB 4, W 2, NB 2)	16
Total		**144**	(1 wicket)	**120**

ENGLAND	O	M	R	W	O	M	R	W
Bedser	38.3	16	55	7	17.2	7	44	7
Bailey	44	14	75	2	5	1	28	0
Wardle	35	16	55	1	12	3	24	0
Tattersall	23	5	59	0	5	0	22	3

AUSTRALIA								
Lindwall	20.4	2	57	5	16	4	37	0
Johnston	18	7	22	0	18	9	14	0
Hill	19	8	35	3	12	3	26	1
Davidson	15	7	22	2	5	1	7	0
Benaud					5	0	15	0
Morris					2	0	5	0

Umpires: D. Davies and H. Elliot.

ENGLAND v AUSTRALIA 1953 (2nd Test)
Played at Lords, on 25-30 June.
Toss: Australia.　　　Result: MATCH DRAWN.

AUSTRALIA

A.L. Hassett*	c Bailey b Bedser	104	c Evans b Statham	3
A.R. Morris	st Evans b Bedser	30	c Statham b Compton	89
R.N. Harvey	lbw b Bedser	59	b Bedser	21
K.R. Miller	b Wardle	25	b Wardle	109
G.B. Hole	c Compton b Wardle	13	lbw b Brown	47
R. Benaud	lbw b Wardle	0	c Graveney b Bedser	5
A.K. Davidson	c Statham b Bedser	76	c and b Brown	15
D.T. Ring	lbw b Wardle	18	lbw b Brown	7
R.R. Lindwall	b Statham	9	b Bedser	50
G.R. Langley+	c Watson b Bedser	1	b Brown	9
W.A. Johnston	not out	3	not out	0
Extras	(B 4, LB 4)	8	(B 8, LB 5)	13
Total		**346**		**368**

ENGLAND

L. Hutton*	c Hole b Johnston	145	c Hole b Lindwall	5
D. Kenyon	c Davidson b Lindwall	3	c Hassett b Lindwall	2
T.W. Graveney	b Lindwall	78	c Langley b Johnston	2
D.S. Compton	c Hole b Benaud	57	lbw b Johnston	33
W. Watson	st Langley b Johnston	4	c Hole b Ring	109
T.E. Bailey	c and b Miller	2	c Benaud b Ring	71
F.R. Brown	c Langley b Lindwall	22	c Hole b Benaud	28
T.G. Evans+	b Lindwall	0	not out	11
J.H. Wardle	b Davidson	23	not out	0
A.V. Bedser	b Lindwall	1		
J.B. Statham	not out	17		
Extras	(B 11,LB 1,W 1,NB 7)	20	(B 7,LB 6,W 2,NB 6)	21
Total		**372**	(7 wickets)	**282**

ENGLAND	O	M	R	W	O	M	R	W
Bedser	42.4	8	105	5	31.5	8	77	3
Statham	28	7	48	1	15	3	40	1
Brown	25	7	53	0	27	4	82	4
Bailey	16	2	55	0	10	4	24	0
Wardle	29	8	77	4	46	18	111	1
Compton					3	0	21	1

AUSTRALIA								
Lindwall	23	4	66	5	19	3	26	2
Miller	25	6	57	1	17	8	17	0
Johnston	35	11	91	2	29	10	70	2
Ring	14	2	43	0	29	5	84	2
Benaud	19	4	70	1	17	6	51	1
Davidson	10.5	2	25	1	14	5	13	0
Hole					1	1	0	0

Umpires: H.G.Baldwin and F.S. Lee.

ENGLAND v AUSTRALIA 1953 (3rd Test)
Played at Old Trafford, Manchester, on 9-14 July.
Toss Australia.   Result: MATCH DRAWN

AUSTRALIA

A.L. Hassett*	b Bailey	26	c Bailey b Bedser	8
A.R. Morris	b Bedser	1	c Hutton b Laker	0
K.R. Miller	b Bedser	17	st Evans b Laker	6
R.N. Harvey	c Evans b Bedser	122	b Wardle	0
G.B. Hole	c Evans b Bedser	66	c Evans b Bedser	2
J.H. de Courcy	lbw b Wardle	41	st Evans b Wardle	8
A.K. Davidson	st Evans b Laker	15	not out	4
R.G. Archer	c Compton b Bedser	5	lbw b Wardle	0
R.R. Lindwall	c Edrich b Wardle	1	b Wardle	4
J.C. Hill	not out	8	not out	0
G.R.A. Langley+	c Edrich b Wardle	8		
Extras	(B 6,LB 1,NB 1)	8	(LB 3)	3
Total		**318**	**(8 wickets)**	**35**

ENGLAND

L. Hutton*	lbw b Lindwall	66
W.J. Edrich	c Hole b Hill	6
T.W. Graveney	c de Courcy b Miller	5
D.S. Compton	c Langley b Archer	45
J.H. Wardle	b Lindwall	5
W. Watson	b Davidson	16
R.T. Simpson	c Langley b Davidson	31
T.E. Bailey	c Hole b Hill	27
T.G. Evans+	not out	44
J.C. Laker	lbw b Hill	5
A.V. Bedser	b Morris	10
Extras	(B 8,LB 8)	16
Total		**276**

ENGLAND	O	M	R	W	O	M	R	W
Bedser	45	10	115	5	4	1	14	2
Bailey	26	4	83	1				
Wardle	28.3	10	70	3	5	2	7	4
Laker	17	3	42	1	9	5	11	2

AUSTRALIA	O	M	R	W
Lindwall	20	8	30	2
Archer	15	8	12	1
Hill	35	7	97	3
Miller	24	11	38	1
Davidson	20	4	60	2
Harvey	3	2	2	0
Hole	2	0	16	0
Morris	1	0	5	1

Umpires: D. Davies and H. Elliot.

ENGLAND v AUSTRALIA 1953 (4th Test)
Played at Headingley, Leeds, on 23-28 July
Toss: Australia.   Result: MATCH DRAWN.

ENGLAND

L. Hutton*	b Lindwall	0	c Langley b Archer	25
W.J. Edrich	lbw b Miller	10	c de Courcy b Lindwall	64
T.W. Graveney	c Benaud b Miller	55	b Lindwall	3
D.S. Compton	c Davidson b Lindwall	0	lbw b Lindwall	61
W. Watson	b Lindwall	24	c Davidson b Miller	15
R.T. Simpson	c Langley b Lindwall	15	c de Courcy b Miller	0
T.E. Bailey	run out	7	c Hole b Davidson	38
T.G.Evans+	lbw b Lindwall	25	c Lindwall b Miller	1
J.C. Laker	c Lindwall b Archer	10	c Benaud b Davidson	48
G.A.R. Lock	b Davidson	9	c Morris b Miller	8
A.V. Bedser	not out	0	not out	3
Extras	(B 8,LB 4)	12	(B 1,LB 8)	9
Total		**167**		**275**

AUSTRALIA

A.L. Hassett*	c Lock b Bedser	37	b Lock	4
A.R. Morris	c Lock b Bedser	10	st Evans b Laker	38
R.N. Harvey	lbw b Bailey	71	lbw b Bedser	34
K.R. Miller	c Edrich b Bailey	5		
G.B. Hole	c Lock b Bedser	53	c Graveney b Bailey	33
J.H. de Courcy	lbw b Lock	10	not out	13
R. Benaud	b Bailey	7		
A.K. Davidson	c Evans b Bedser	2	not out	17
R.G. Archer	not out	31		
R.R. Lindwall	b Bedser	9		
G.R.A. Langley+	c Hutton b Bedser	17		
Extras	(B 4,LB 8,W 2)	14	(B 3,LB 4,W 1)	8
Total		**266**	(4 wickets)	**147**

AUSTRALIA	O	M	R	W	O	M	R	W
Lindwall	35	10	54	5	54	19	104	3
Miller	28	13	39	2	47	19	63	4
Davidson	20.4	7	23	1	29.3	15	36	2
Archer	18	4	27	1	25	12	31	1
Benaud	8	1	12	0	19	8	26	0
Hole					3	1	6	0

ENGLAND								
Bedser	28.5	2	95	6	17	1	65	1
Bailey	22	4	71	3	6	1	9	1
Lock	23	9	53	1	8	1	48	1
Laker	9	1	33	0	2	0	17	1

Umpires: F. Chester and F.S. Lee.

ENGLAND v AUSTRALIA 1953 (5th Test)
Played at Kennington Oval, London, on 15-19 August.
Toss: Australia.   Result: ENGLAND won by eight wickets.

AUSTRALIA

A.L. Hassett*	c Evans b Bedser	53	lbw b Laker	10
A.R. Morris	lbw b Bedser	16	lbw b Lock	26
K.R. Miller	lbw b Bailey	1	c Trueman b Laker	0
R.N. Harvey	c Hutton b Trueman	36	b Lock	1
G.B. Hole	c Evans b Trueman	37	lbw b Laker	17
J.H. de Courcy	c Evans b Trueman	5	run out	4
R.G. Archer	c and b Bedser	10	c Edrich b Lock	49
A.K. Davidson	c Edrich b Laker	22	b Lock	21
R.R. Lindwall	c Evans b Trueman	62	c Compton b Laker	12
G.R. Langley+	c Edrich b Lock	18	c Trueman b Lock	2
W.A. Johnston	not out	9	not out	6
Extras	(B 4,NB 2)	6	(B 11,LB 3)	14
Total		**275**		**162**

ENGLAND

L. Hutton*	b Johnston	82	run out	17
W.J. Edrich	lbw b Lindwall	21	not out	55
P.B.H. May	c Archer b Johnston	39	c Davidson b Miller	37
D.S. Compton	c Langley b Lindwall	16	not out	22
T.W. Graveney	c Miller b Lindwall	4		
T.E. Bailey	b Archer	64		
T.G. Evans+	run out	28		
J.C. Laker	c Langley b Miller	1		
G.A.R. Lock	c Davidson b Lindwall	4		
F.S. Trueman	b Johnston	10		
A.V. Bedser	not out	22		
Extras	(B 9,LB 5, W 1)	15	(LB 1)	1
Total		**306**	(2 wickets)	**132**

ENGLAND	O	M	R	W	O	M	R	W
Bedser	29	3	88	3	11	2	24	0
Trueman	24.3	3	86	4	2	1	4	0
Bailey	14	3	42	1				
Lock	9	2	19	1	21	9	45	5
Laker	5	0	34	1	16.5	2	75	4

AUSTRALIA	O	M	R	W	O	M	R	W
Lindwall	32	7	70	4	21	5	46	0
Miller	34	12	65	1	11	3	24	1
Johnston	45	16	94	3	19	14	52	0
Davidson	10	1	26	0				
Archer	10.3	2	25	1	1	1	0	0
Hole	11	6	11	0				
Hassett					1	0	4	0
Morris					0.5	0	5	0

Umpires: D. Davies and F.S. Lee

Sir Leonard Hutton
Born Fulneck, Pudsey, Yorkshire, on 23 June, 1916.
Died Kingston, Surrey, 6 September, 1990.

FIRST CLASS CAREER

Batting	M.	Inns	No	Runs	H.S.	Av.
	513	814	91	40,140	364	55.51

Centuries	129

Fifties	179

Hutton lies 14th in the present list of most runs scored in first class cricket.
He is 8th in the list of most centuries scored.

Innings over 200

v Derbyshire	Sheffield, 1937	271 not out
v Australia	The Oval, 1938	364
v E. Province	P. Elizabeth 1938-9	202
v Hampshire	Sheffield, 1939	280 not out
v Hampshire	Bournemouth, 1947	270 not out
v Northants	Wellingborough, 1949	269 not out
v New Zealand	The Oval, 1949	206
v Lancashire	Old Trafford, 1949	201
v West Indies	The Oval, 1950	202 not out
v Gentlemen	Scarborough, 1953	241
v West Indies	Jamaica, 1953-4	205

Hutton scored 1000 runs in a season 17 times and 3000 runs once, in 1949.
In the same year he scored 1294 runs in June, more than any other player has
ever scored in one month in first class cricket.

Bowling	Runs	Wickets	Average
	5,106	173	29.51

He has taken ten wickets in a match once and five wickets in an innings four times.
His best bowling return was 6 for 76.

Catches	400

TEST RECORD

Batting	M.	Inns	No	Runs	H.S.	Av.
	79	138	15	6971	364	56.67

Centuries	19

Fifties	33

Only Boycott, Cowdrey, Gower and Hammond have scored more runs in Test cricket than Hutton, and they have played in 108, 114 ,109 and 85 matches respectively, as compared to Hutton's 79. His average places him 6th in the list of Englishmen in Test matches, while his innings of 364 has still only been surpassed once in the history of Test cricket.
He also holds the English record for both 1st and 2nd wicket partnerships in Test cricket.
The former is 359 with C. Washbrook and the latter 382 with M. Leyland.

Bowling	Runs	Wickets	Average
	232	3	77.33

Best bowling: 1 for 2.

Catches	57

Picture acknowledgements

The Hulton Picture Company:
p18, p20, p23, p24 (bottom), p25, p26 (bottom), p29 (right), p32,
p37, p38 (right), p41, p42 (bottom), p44 (top and bottom), p45,
p46 (top and bottom), p47 (top), p48, p49 (top right and bottom),
p50, p52, p53, p55, p56, p59 (bottom), p60, p61 (top and bottom),
p62 (top and bottom), p63, p64 (top), p66, p67 (top and bottom),
p69, p70, p72 (bottom), p73 (top and bottom), p74 (top and
bottom), p75 (top and bottom), p76 (top and bottom), p77, p79,
p81 (top and bottom), p82, p83, p84 (top and bottom), p87,
p88 (left), p91 (top), p95.

Allsport:
p17 (right), p34, p72 (top), p90, p94, p96 and the photograph on
the front jacket cover.

Ken Kelly:
p26 (top), p30, p36 (top), p49 (top left), p57, p71, p86, p93 (right).

USPA:
p14.